Reviews for 18 Steps to an All-Star LinkedIn Profile

Working with Andrea motivated me, she actually made me a social media practitioner. I love it.

18 Steps to an All Star LinkedIn Profile is truthful, simple and efficient. If you don't feel like starting to work on your social media skills after reading it, you will end up feeling guilty not doing so.

The book translates Andrea's energy and passion for people through social media, as she is willing to make anyone of us shine in our own ways. LinkedIn is simply the best way to start, I can imagine more suggestion coming from Andrea, brace yourself!!!!

Julian Kasparian
CEO, BNP Paribas Securities Services,
Hong Kong

Andrea is my digital angel. She opened my eyes to the possibility of LinkedIn and more broadly on social media, showing me the huge potential for business professionals. When it comes to understanding how to use LinkedIn with integrity and power, Andrea Edwards and *18 Steps* should be your first port of call.

Stanimira Koleva
Senior Vice President and General Manager,
Here Technologies, Asia Pacific and Japan

Andrea is leading the digital battle of good against mediocre when it comes to social leadership. This is the starting point everyone needs to just get done, because from here, you'll start to see the true power social leadership brings, not just to yourself, but to your business. Andrea has been a key partner in this transformation for my company. I suggest you listen to her.

Nishan Weerasinghe
CMO, Fortune 500 MNC,
Asia Top 50 Marketer

Andrea is totally passionate about the business and personal benefits of social leadership. She has been a leader in this space for many years and has kept up and refined her approach as the industry has changed. I have seen her share her advice and inspire groups with her energy for the subject.

The advice she shares in *18 Steps to an All-Star LinkedIn Profile* is simple to put in place yet highly effective and recommended if you want to see business results.

Michelle Cockrill
Head of Marketing and Communications,
BNP Paribas Securities Services APAC

Andrea's ability to break down how to get started on your social leadership journey is outstanding. I've shared variations of this information across my internal and external networks more times than I can count. Andrea's passion for social leadership and her ability to relate the results to business outcomes is what motivates many people I know to finally get started. But more than that, they believe it's worth the time to invest in creating value—not noise—across their own networks. Thank you for continuing to lead and inspire all of us to do differently.

Wendy McEwan
marketing and business executive
working across Asia

I know when I first started on social media, it was photos of what I ate and where I was. My friends were the same. As time moved on, I observed connections who were able to position themselves as someone to listen to; they had something important to share and were very clear on who they were, personally and in business. So, I asked myself—how does that picture of a coffee or odd-looking cat jump that ravine and become something of importance to other people?

Andrea's book, *18 Steps to an All Star LinkedIn Profile* showed me. Andrea has eloquently—and without fuss—taken away the fear and loathing from putting yourself out there and making YOURSELF the brand. Her step-by-step approach is a real-world way to get your voice, brand and message out there without the "preach."

Sinisa Nikolic
Director, AP Cognitive Systems,
Fortune 500 MNC

Andrea has written a must-read primer for anyone taking their first step towards creating a brand for themselves on LinkedIn. As my first guide in this regard, Andrea, her workshop, and *18 Steps* definitely set me on the right track on my personal branding journey. Read this book—and learn from one of the best.

Thariyan Chacko
Group Manager,
Microsoft

There are many people advising you to be more active on LinkedIn, but very few tell you how to be more active and why. This book—in 18 steps—will help you kick-start your journey on LinkedIn and provides honest guidance on how you can share your true passion, unleashing the digital leader in you. If you have a lot of knowledge or are passionate to make a positive impact in the world, then start here.

Deepthi Anne
co-founder of TechAthena
Solution Architect, Fortune 500 MNC

What I love most about Andrea Edwards' timely book is that is provides executives, managers and thought leaders with a step-by-step guide on how to succeed using LinkedIn while at the same time ensuring that quality and integrity are central to your social media strategy. A much-needed handbook which will help you cut through the noise and make a bigger impact in the world. Highly recommended.

James Taylor M.B.A. F.R.S.A.
Keynote Speaker on Business Creativity,
Innovation and Artificial Intelligence

Why do I need to learn it and *who* do I need to learn it from? These are two questions I ask myself when choosing what to read or study. Having an effective LinkedIn profile is going to help you sell yourself, influence your stakeholders, and have conversations with people you would never normally be able to reach. I know this because I've done it, and the person that "kicked my butt" to get it done was Andrea Edwards. There's no better thought-leader when it comes to digital conversations and social media.

Andrew Bryant CSP
author, *Self Leadership*

Andrea's book got me in the first sentence. 'What is social leadership? It's you!' Wow. Straight to the point. Her writing style pulls no punches and it sets the direction of her very practical and insights driven approach on how and why social leadership is so important, and, more importantly, HOW to do it through the platform where a third of the world's professionals hangout. LinkedIn. A must read for anyone serious about being heard, seen and making a difference in this beautiful, chaotic world we call home.

Natalie Turner
author, *Yes, You Can Innovate*,
inventor of The Six 'I's of Innovation.

Everyone talks about LinkedIn, but here is your chance to truly do it well by reading *18 Steps* and putting it into action. Andrea provides a powerful approach to LinkedIn that every executive should use to get ahead. Get started now and let your brand stand out!

Jerome Joseph, CSP
author, *The Brand Playbook*,
global speaker and brand strategist

There are many people who profess that they are a social media specialist, yet they don't practice what they preach. If you're looking for a person that is the best in the business and who walks the talk, then Andrea Edwards, The Digital Conversationalist, is the person you need to learn from.

In her new book, *18 Steps to an All Star LinkedIn Profile*, Andrea walks the reader through the ins and outs of why you need to be on social media and then teaches you step-by-step what you need to do—and how—to create an impactful profile.

If you've never met Andrea, I can tell you, she's the real deal.

Pamela Wigglesworth
CEO, Experiential Hands-on Learning,
author, *The 50-60 Something Start-up Entrepreneur*

I remember Andrea stating to me and others: *never outsource your voice*. This stuck with me and I fired my social media manager. If anyone I know understands social media, it is Andrea. She thoroughly gets what it takes to build a great social media presence, especially on LinkedIn. In *18 Steps*, she gives an outright, honest, no-nonsense account of the steps to take on how to make the most of LinkedIn—especially if you're a beginner! She is my social media guru. Why? Because she debunks the LinkedIn myths and doesn't fluff it up. She tells it beautifully how it is in a super generous way. I recommend you read this transforming book today. It will change your view of LinkedIn and, most of all, how to gain from this B2B platform. Don't outsource your voice, insource your voice.

Kevin Cottam
author, *The Nomadic Mindset*

Andrea unplugs social media and takes a deep dive into the importance of understanding its relevance when building relationships both internally and externally for business. One read of this gem will set leaders and employees on a journey of personal empowerment that will certainly impact their long-term professional fulfilment.

John Gordon
CEO, ExpatChoice.Asia

LinkedIn is such an essential tool in business today and having an all-star LinkedIn profile is essential if you want to stand out from the crowd and do business with just the right people. Andrea Edwards, The Digital Conversationalist, has written the ultimate guide to creating that perfect profile in *18 Steps*. She gives practical, step-by-step tips on how to improve your profile to enable you to shine. I've already gone and given my page on LinkedIn a tune-up following Andrea's insights.

Lindsay Adams
The Relationships Guy

Andrea Edwards is THE guru of LinkedIn. Her extensive experience helps clearly convey the essentials needed to become a real STAR on LinkedIn. This book is all you need to get started.

What I find most appealing about Andrea Edwards is her down-to-earth way of writing, her unflagging determination to help people get over their hesitancy online so they discover their unique talents and gifts, and to support them in getting their voices out into the world. Andrea's book will help you get your message to work.

We can all change the world for the better, just like Andrea. Read this and get started...

Cathy Johnson
The Authenticity Coach

18 Steps to an All Star LinkedIn Profile is packed with practical gems that will help you elevate your personal brand. Andrea leads powerfully by example and brings tremendous clarity to the process of developing social leadership. This book is your personal coach, inspiring you to take action. Highly recommended!

Karen Leong
Author, *Win People Over*,
Founding Director of Influence Solutions

Social media can be confusing, particularly for senior management teams. How can you show authenticity, be true to your corporate brand, and continue to add value? Too often social media is treated like a free space for adverts! Andrea Edwards has the experience and credibility to show you what actually works.

Andrea continues to embody what is needed on social media and, in particular, LinkedIn. Professional and personal positioning with the Goldilocks approach—not too little, not too much, but just right. Using Andrea's advice as mapped out in this book will   put you well ahead of your competition and, to be frank, you would be crazy not to   buy this book and follow it religiously.

Warwick Merry CSP
master MC and success speaker

This book is simply brilliant. Andrea shares important, practical information in an easy-to-read manner—with glimpses of her wonderful sense of humour and passion for leading sustainable, positive change. It's simple, essential, and easy to implement as you read through—in a style relevant to you and your industry. If you want to be a great connector, you need this book!

Kerrie Phipps
author, *Do Talk to Strangers*

18 STEPS
TO AN ALL-STAR
LinkedIn
PROFILE

HOW TO GET STARTED ON LinkedIn

ANDREA T EDWARDS

For every book bought, I plant a tree

Notion Press

Old No. 38, New No. 6
McNichols Road, Chetpet
Chennai - 600 031

First Published by Notion Press 2020
Copyright © Andrea T Edwards 2020
All Rights Reserved.

ISBN 978-1-64760-670-1

This book is dedicated to my love, Steve Johnson.

When you commit to sharing your life with someone,
there's always a lot of give and take.
Agreeing to do that with someone deeply invested
in the digital world, adds a whole other dimension to a
marriage ☺.
You're not an "Instagram husband" my love,
but I really do appreciate you for being by my side
through it all. You're the best of the best xxxxx

Why Social Leadership?

It's you – **amplified!**
It's what you stand for.
It's what you believe in.
It's how you think.
It's how you act.

It is the packaging up of all of YOU, which you then
actively and passionately share with the world online,
driven by a goal of creating change—
in mindset, behavior, or ways of doing things.

What social leadership looks like is different for each of us.
Our job is to identify the magic within and then
unleash it digitally.

Once we identify our personal magic—
which we already celebrate in the physical world,
a much smaller stage—
today we have the opportunity to amplify it across a larger
and
more impactful digital world.

And when we have something powerful to share,
something that can change lives, enhance professional
careers, or make the world a better place,
it's selfish to hold it back.

In today's digital and physical world,
when we own our voice, we own our future!
@AndreaTEdwards

Contents

A Quick Introduction to Social Leadership........................1

    What I Know to be True..1

    The Benefits are Enormous—for You and Your
    Business 5

    Social Media is Where Customers are Today 8

A Few Introductory Thoughts on LinkedIn......................11

    Pick Your Platform 11

    We Are All Responsible for LinkedIn 14

    My Suggested Strategy?..16

    Why is LinkedIn Important? 18

    Dog Ear This Page for Later......................................21

    Know Your Social Selling Index (SSI)......................23

    Establish Your Professional Brand 26

    Find the Right People 27

    Engage With Insights and Build Relationships.....29

    How Do You Compare with Your Peers? 30

    Before You Do Anything, Do This 32

    Why These 18 Steps, Why Now?.............................34

Contents

The 18 Steps to an All-Star LinkedIn Profile 35

1 – Set Up Your Profile Properly 37

2 – Create a Unique Web Address 42

3 – Add Your Photo and Banner 44

4 – Write Your Professional Headline 50

5 – Write Your Summary 56

6 – Cover Your History, Update
Your Positions 62

7 – Follow Companies, the Media, and
Influencers 65

8 – Use Hashtags 69

9 – Include People, Businesses, and
Publications in Your Posts 79

10 – Send Two Recommendations Today 83

11 – List Your Skills 85

12 – Are You Looking for a Job? 88

13 – Use LinkedIn Groups 90

14 – List The Causes You Care About and
Promote the Ones You Volunteer For 95

15 – Have You Been Published Anywhere? 97

16 – Add Honors, Awards, and Associations 99

17 – Go Premium 100

18 – Final Tips On LinkedIn 103

Be Amazing..105

    Things You Can Do to Keep Lifting
    Your Profile..108

Andrea T Edwards, CSP *113*
Acknowledgements *115*

A Quick Introduction to Social Leadership

What I Know to be True

Building a strong, powerful social leadership position and really owning your voice is how you build your future. Whatever you want to do, whatever you hope to achieve, whatever path you have mapped out for your life, you can get there by connecting to others on social media and by intelligently participating, with deep integrity and authenticity, in community conversations. By building your social leadership presence, you cement yourself as an expert in your field. You become the go-to person, the master of your domain.

In a world undergoing cataclysmic change across all aspects of life, we must consider our social media presence as one of the most important career-building tools at our disposal today. Think of it as health insurance for your career. However, YOU must embrace it and get started. No one will do this for you. It's your voice, and only you can best represent you.

Not enough professionals take their social leadership presence seriously today, and the way people interact with social media is rapidly changing. As social media takes an ever more central place in our collective political, economic, and emotional lives, the only way to avoid being left behind is to establish your presence early and cultivate it with agility and sensitivity to evolving trends.

Not only can social leadership dramatically change your career path, personal opportunities, and profile, it will also build and change your business—or the business you work for—in such fundamental ways. You'll wonder why you waited! This is happening—now.

Employee advocacy is a hot topic these days and your employer will expect you to build your profile soon, if they haven't asked you already. Take control by getting out in front, without buying into the current employee advocacy message. *Own* your own social leadership. Employee advocacy is about the company you work for. Social leadership is about you, with benefits to your employer as a happy, symbiotic secondary effect. This a very important distinction.

It comes down to this: don't allow the company you work for to control your profile. Your profile is yours, and you shouldn't delegate or outsource it to anyone. There is enough noise out there, and the majority of current employee advocacy programs are highly ineffective.

It's time for all of us to step up and become social leaders, with a mindset of serving our audience in a meaningful and authentic way. You can only achieve this by participating and getting your hands dirty. You can't understand social media or gauge its value from the outside, looking in.

Only true engagement by listening, participating, and leading—on the relevant platforms used daily by your audience—will unlock those insights and allow you to have meaningful impact.

Important takeaways:

1. It's not scary or hard. You don't need to invest huge amounts of time.

2. It's all about the quality of content you create and/ or share.

3. Getting focused is the most critical part of being successful.

4. It's about creating a habit of giving to and serving your community by sharing knowledge that can change lives and businesses. A social leader understands it's not about self-promotion, but about giving value to their audience.

Social leadership, quite simply, is an act of service.

McKinsey's 2013 report, "Six social-media skills every leader needs," found that any company that develops a **critical mass** of leaders who master the skills of social media will experience significant business benefits. This is as true today.

Here are some of those business benefits according to McKinsey, along with my own edits and additions:[1]

- Being more creative, innovative, and agile;

- Attracting and retaining the best talent;

- Tapping deeper into the capabilities and ideas of employees and stakeholders;

---

1. "Six social-media skills every leader needs," McKinsey Quarterly, Roland Deiser and Sylvain Newton, February 2013.

- Becoming more effective at collaborating across internal and external boundaries;

- Enjoying a higher degree of global integration— which is critical for the future of borderless business;

- Creating more loyal customer relationships, leading to greater brand equity;

- Playing an industry leadership role by leveraging partners to co-create, co-develop, and collaborate;

- Being more likely to create new business models that capitalize on the potential of evolving communication technologies;

- Empowering your business to confront the shortcomings of traditional organizational design;

- Addressing shortcomings to develop infrastructure that underpins strategic use of social technologies;

- Initiating a positive loop, allowing individuals and businesses to capitalize on the opportunities and disruptions that come with the community of a networked society; and

- Gaining the rewards of new competitive advantage.

Considering this paper was published in 2013, and that the benefits of a critical mass of leaders embracing social media are phenomenal, it's surprising to still see so few leaders and businesses really engaging in social leadership as we begin the 2020s.

The Benefits are Enormous—for You and Your Business

Adopting a social leadership presence will change the way you think. It will change the way you work. When it becomes a strategic priority for your business, it will harness the voice of your team members to transform your business from the inside out. It creates a people-focused culture that benefits everyone within your community. It is the core tool of innovation in business today, because it is about communication—the essence of being human.

A social leadership culture breaks down hierarchies and silos. It positions all employees as externally focused (rather than the internal focus so common today in corporate culture) and it empowers all employees in a business—not just those at the very top. If you want to build trust, social leadership opens that door.

Overstating it? I am not.

Over the last three years, I have had the privilege of working with IBM across Asia Pacific. We have a full 24-month track record demonstrating business value and employee wins.

This data is based on interviews and responses from a survey of 70 IBM employees. The data is shared with IBM's authorisation in a full case study[2] published with IBM. This is their view on what happened when they made social leadership a priority.

- Pipeline generated directly from social media in 2017 was US$57 + million and US$140 million in 2018 = 145% growth

- Wins in 2017 were US$24 million and in 2018 it went up to US$40 million = 66% growth

The top five benefits highlighted by employees:

1. Clients learning about IBM from the content I am sharing = 54%

2. Growing belief in the effectiveness of strategic social selling = 52%

3. I am learning more as I create content and actively seek world-class content to share with my networks = 49%

4. Bigger networks globally, opening doors to opportunities for IBM and myself = 48%

5. Believe IBM is on the right track as a business of the future = 38%

Hard to achieve? Definitely not. They began with the 18 Steps.

The one thing I hear from professionals and C-suite leaders all the time is that *they want to do it, but they want to do it well.* They don't want to look foolish or out of step with social media's rapidly changing technologies and culture.

---

2. https://www.slideshare.net/AndreaTEdwards/success-story-unleash-your-employees-disrupt-from-within-grow-your-business-103390123

In working with IBM and other multinational organizations, I hear these challenges repeated often. I'm sharing so you, as a leader, can address them.

Six key challenges that hold employees back from social leadership:

1. Self-confidence—"Why would anyone care what I have to say?"

2. Employees cannot see the benefit to themselves personally—happy with their career path as it is.

3. Time commitment is a barrier, even with simple steps identified, such as posting one article per week that's aligned to your focus on LinkedIn.

4. Their managers are not embracing social leadership, and employees lack support. Leadership buy-in is critical.

5. Perceived as a waste of time by peers who have not embraced social leadership, so employees struggle with feeling this work is not valued. It's a culture change that starts from the top.

6. Many employees struggle with the idea that successful social leadership requires more long-term engagement and persistence than they can commit to.

It all starts with getting the tools you need in place and then getting focused. This book is about helping you organize your strategy for LinkedIn, the world's biggest online professional network. Most people are stuck—at the beginning. Stick with me through these pages and I will help you move past this barrier and set you up to thrive in the social leadership age.

Social media is more than a LinkedIn profile or a Facebook page. It's more than your friends' lunchtime foodie posts, where they're hanging out right now, what they're doing as they post yet *another* selfie, those annoying motivational memes, or whatever irks you about social media—and there's plenty that's irksome!

What it provides is an opportunity to openly communicate a focused message with our communities and a platform to have discussions with like-minded people. When we do this well on LinkedIn, we change how we do business—and we can even change the world.

The transformative power of social media and content marketing comes into play when it is embraced from the very top of an organization—and then right across it. It is only when every CEO genuinely engages as a social leader, and empowers every employee to do the same, that we will see a fundamental shift in how we do business and how we run our organizations. This shift will make businesses and organizations more successful, more open and more trusted.

It is time for us all to lead socially, to be more authentic, more passionate, and more giving. It is time to open ourselves up, to be vulnerable, to smash down unhelpful hierarchies, and to knock down the PR walls executives have been hiding behind for decades. It is time to join the digital arena, because that's the only place where we can fully understand today's consumers and grow our organizations. It's an age of collaboration, of service, and of engagement, and it's time for you to get out there in the digital world.

If you are reading these words out of a desire to make a change in your life and for your business, whether you're a young professional keen to understand how to build a professional profile to support your career ambitions or a business leader persuaded that your organization can become something more through the power of social media and online content, this book is for you. What we'll get to here is the stuff that creates real business transformation today.

This book is just the starting point. Enjoy the journey with me and put any cynicism in your back pocket, for now. All I ask is that you give me a chance to change your mind—and hopefully inspire you, too.

My next book, *The Social Leadership Manifesto*, will take you deeper into the strategies and tactics that will ensure you are a social leader your industry pays attention to. But first, let's start with the basics and get your LinkedIn profile looking world-class.

Cheers,

Andrea

A Few Introductory Thoughts on LinkedIn

Pick Your Platform

Where do you need to be present on social media to build your professional career? Like all things to do with social media, there is no single answer. When working with professionals across all industries, I say to prioritize LinkedIn first, then Twitter. The statistics are clear: while they are far from the only choices, these are the two professional social platforms of choice for business.

The best place to start is to research social media use in your industry. Ask around if you don't know. Identify your industry leaders. See which platforms they are active on, and you'll have your answer. If you're in an industry slow to embrace social media and you can't find much presence, you have a unique pioneering opportunity to establish the priority social channels for your sector.

Perhaps you are in a creative industry, or maybe you are an educator, a doctor, or a charity worker. The most important question to ask then, depending on what you do and what you want to achieve is this: where is everyone else in your industry? If you're in a visual industry, Instagram is superb. Facebook is also a critical social media platform to be part of, given its scale.

Of course, there may be platforms or ways of using social media that are unique to your country, language, or industry. Examples include WeChat, Weibo, and Line. Or perhaps you will find your leadership opportunity in a more private corner of the internet. Business leaders often set up private, invitation-only communities on LinkedIn, for example. How do you get that invitation? Do you know who owns the group? Does someone in your network belong to it, and can they help you get an invite? The more you build your profile and professional presence, the more invitations you will receive to network and join relevant conversations.

Some industries, such as energy and construction, operate almost exclusively within LinkedIn Groups, as another example of use. Deals are done in these groups, RFPs are shared. Does your industry work that way these days? Ask around to find out.

The way the major platforms are used varies not only by industry, but across different countries. For example, Facebook has a very different role in Indonesia, Thailand, and the Philippines than in Singapore, Australia, and Hong Kong—where it's concerned more with family and community than business-focused. Depending on where you operate, you may need to make Facebook a bigger business priority. Understanding what works in each local market is critical.

Another critical question is where and how you enjoy participating on social media. If you don't enjoy your chosen social media platform, you will never participate with the same passion as you would on a platform you love. So, if you're a business professional who loves Instagram or SnapChat, these will be powerful places for you to build your presence. Look at what other professionals are doing on these platforms and seek inspiration. The most important thing is that you love what you're doing.

For me professionally, it's LinkedIn, Twitter, Facebook, SlideShare, and YouTube. What's in the mix of your ideal social media cocktail?

If, on the other hand, you're barely participating anywhere and you want to start building your credibility as a social leader, you must start with LinkedIn, the international business platform.

It's also time to move beyond the old thinking that LinkedIn is just for recruitment. Today LinkedIn is an enormously influential platform with world-class content and unparalleled networking opportunities. When you find yourself checking LinkedIn on the weekend, as you do other social media, you'll know it has come into its own as a powerful information resource that will help you flourish in your career and industry.

However, for everyone who complains that LinkedIn is flooded with nonsense these days, I have to point out a fundamental truth of social media: LinkedIn, like any platform is only as good as you make it. Invest in it. Create and propagate quality content. Unfollow people or businesses that are not delivering value to you. Over time it will become a powerful resource that will help you be successful and establish your eminence.

You, me, and 660+ million other users are responsible for the quality of LinkedIn. I believe in taking personal responsibility, and this is as true for social media as for any aspect of life. In the spirit of building a better online world for ourselves, it's important we address upfront the fact that LinkedIn is awesome, but it comes with many annoyances.

We've all read threads by people complaining that members of LinkedIn are making Facebook-like posts on what's supposed to be a professional platform. We've seen attractive women posting alluring pictures that garner thousands of comments running the gamut from "Inappropriate!" to "You're so pretty." Naturally, the people who spend their time making such comments have no idea how bad it makes them look, and the people posting the pictures are similarly out of touch—if we're even looking at real accounts. It doesn't take much digging to recognize the many fake accounts out there.

Then there's the connection who is proud their kid has graduated from university after a hard slog. This parent is naturally thrilled about their kid's achievement, and some friends are supportive, but the rest of LinkedIn says, "No, not welcome here." Some of our connections will inevitably post cute videos or memes of animals or share their religious or political views, whereby we quickly express our outrage: "Not on LinkedIn, thank you!"

The posts that concern me the most, though, are people wanting to walk away from LinkedIn because "it's not a good platform anymore." Too much self-promotion. Too much useless information. Too much nonsense. And I agree—there is far too much nonsense on LinkedIn today, but walking away is not the solution. We can and must make it better, together, for all of us.

I believe LinkedIn is an amazing platform, and I have been 100 percent committed to growing my LinkedIn presence for more than a decade. Yes, there's a lot more nonsense going on, but I've developed the ability to filter out the annoyances outlined above:

Pretty girl: ignore these posts or be entertained by the comments without getting involved. Feisty trolls can break up a dull day!

Pets, politics, and religion: I don't approve, but I'm not going to react. Connections making such posts are ignored...

The rest: I simply can't be bothered to care. I'm looking for useful information and if you're wasting my time, I'll give my attention (which is, after all, the most valuable currency on social media) to someone whose posts enrich and inform me.

In general, I encourage you not to take it all too seriously. Getting worked up about what bothers you on social media is a waste of your energy. **Let it go and focus on being awesome yourself, and on making the conversations you engage in meaningful.** That's something you can do.

Focus on being the best version of yourself on LinkedIn and across all social media. Ask yourself: Are you delivering information that will bring value to your audience? Are you celebrating people in your networks by engaging with them or praising them for a job well done? Are your regularly writing someone a recommendation?

Build stronger filters and blank out the nonsense. If you see someone participating on LinkedIn in a way you think is inappropriate, don't comment—with one click you can remove them from your world. It's very easy. Let them figure out that if they're consistently posting foolishly, their connections start dropping off.

Is your messaging inbox on LinkedIn full of sales nonsense? This can make it impossible to keep track of the messages you actually want to read. So, reply and challenge them: "Why did you send this to me? Did you review my profile first?" I can guarantee 99 percent of senders will not respond, but you won't get spam from them again, either!

If you have connections who are participating inappropriately and you know them personally, talk to them. The best way to lead is by example, but some people are stubborn or just lacking in observation skills and awareness of their own impact. Talk to them and help them be better. They won't all hear you, but at least you tried to approach them from an angle of service. You can unfriend as needed. We really do have a shared responsibility on LinkedIn—and all social media—to make it better.

Be kind, always. There is enough nasty stuff going on in the world right now and personally, I don't differentiate between violent behavior in the "real" world and people ripping each other to shreds on social media. Nastiness is nastiness. We need more givers, not haters, if we want to make the world a better place.

LinkedIn has done an amazing job building a world-class content platform, and it's only going to keep growing and evolving, but we all have to play our part. That means we must all be focused on being awesome by delivering value to our communities, lifting others up, and using the platform as if it were the best version of itself—a tool to build our dreams and make them come true.

It's powerful stuff.

At the moment, LinkedIn is *the* professional platform on social media. It's absolutely critical to understand the many ways you can use it and the features available (on a platform that's always evolving and mostly getting better), as well as how to participate in a meaningful way. Don't underestimate its power, even if you don't admire how other people use it. Don't worry about them—your job is to outshine them.

Reasons to use LinkedIn—let's look at the data:

- One third of professionals on the planet are on LinkedIn.

- There are well over 660 million members, which equates to two new members every second.

- There are 110 industries across 200 countries and territories represented.

- More than 30 million companies are represented on LinkedIn.

- Seventy percent of users are now outside of the US.

- LinkedIn is currently available in 24 languages: Arabic, English, Simplified Chinese, Traditional Chinese, Czech, Danish, Dutch, French, German, Indonesian, Italian, Japanese, Korean, Malay, Norwegian, Polish, Portuguese, Romanian, Russian, Spanish, Swedish, Tagalog, Thai, and Turkish.

- There are more than 46 million students and recent college graduates on LinkedIn. They represent LinkedIn's fastest-growing demographic.

- It is the most affluent social network.

- Sixty-one percent of members use it as their primary professional network.

- Ninety-four percent of journalists and editors use it.

- Key decision-makers make up 49 percent of LinkedIn members.

- It is truly global and not censored in countries where other social platforms are limited.

- Google loves LinkedIn. When searching for your name, don't be surprised if your LinkedIn profile is the first suggestion.

Let's break the numbers of users down world-wide[3]:

206+ million in Europe,
181+ million in North America
175+ million in Asia and the Pacific
95+ million in Latin America
31+ million in the Middle East, and Africa

---

3. Current LinkedIn stats can be found at https://news.linkedin.com/about-us#statistics.

Learn from those who inspire you

Make a list of 10 people you admire on LinkedIn (or any social media platform) and review their profiles. Pay attention to how they actively participate. Take notes on what makes them stand out, as well as how they implement the strategies we'll discuss in the following pages. You will stand out if you watch, learn, and listen from the best of what social media has to offer.

Many professionals fail to make time for this simple reflection in advance, which means they are missing an opportunity to think about what makes a powerful online presence *pop*. Spend some time on this exercise and you will be off to an excellent start.

Notes—my list of 10 professional social media profiles that I admire and want to learn from

1.
2.
3.
4.
5.
6.
7.
8.
9.
10.

Dog Ear This Page
for Later

Character limits on LinkedIn

Before we continue, mark this page to refer back to later as you implement the advice in the following sections. When you start building your LinkedIn profile, it's really important to understand character limits, or the number of letters (not words) you can use for each section. This character count includes spaces. If you know the limit upfront, you'll be able to create content tailored to the confines of that space, which will save you time once you're uploading those texts. Try to use the maximum number of characters allowed; it's your story, and there's a lot to tell.

The information here is correct at time of writing (always subject to change):

- Professional headline: 120 characters

- Professional summary: 2,000 characters

- Your website anchor text: 30 characters

- Website URL: 256 characters

- Position title: 100 characters

- Position description: 200 minimum, or up to 2,000 characters

- Interests: 1,000 characters

- Skills: you can include up to 50 skills, using 61 characters per skill

- LinkedIn status update: up to 700 characters; the first 140 characters are visible; the rest are hidden by the **see more** button.

Creating text with these limits in mind will save you time later, I promise. For all of the latest information on LinkedIn, check out the LinkedIn help page.[4] Ask questions and hopefully you'll get your answers.

Drafting my 120 characters

Experiment here

1. _____

_____

2. _____

_____

3. _____

_____

---

4.   https://www.linkedin.com/help/linkedin

Know Your Social
Selling Index (SSI)

LinkedIn has created what they call the Social Selling Index (SSI) to measure the key elements of successful LinkedIn participation.

Before updating your LinkedIn profile, it's important to know where your reputation really is on the platform. LinkedIn tracks four key metrics to help you see how effective you are at 1) establishing your professional brand, 2) finding the right people, 3) engaging with insights, and 4) building relationships. These four categories combine to make your Social Selling Index.

How Do You Find it?

Open a new window and type www.linkedin.com/sales/ssi into the URL bar. Because this is a separate page, you won't be able to access it through your LinkedIn profile. You, however, will need to log on to LinkedIn to see your result, which means you need to have your password handy.

Here is a recent screen shot of my SSI with a rating of 90, which puts me in the top one percent of my network. Considering what I do, I would expect a rating within this range. Likewise, when we take a look at the SSIs of LinkedIn sales professionals (i.e. sales people working for LinkedIn), many of them have a score of 92+, which we would expect from a social seller working for a social media company.

Social Selling Dashboard   Share your SSI ↗

Andrea Edwards - The Digi...
Helping businessess and professionals
tell better stories, while rousing passions   Top 1%   Top 1%
in people to embrace social leadership   Industry SSI Rank   Network SSI Rank

Social Selling Index - Today
Your Social Selling Index (SSI) measures how effective you are at establishing your professional
brand, finding the the right people, engaging with insights, and building relationships.
It is updated daily. **Learn more**

90
out of 100

Establish your professional brand		24,5
	0	25
Find the right people		20.24
	0	25
Engage with insights		19.88
	0	25
Build relationships		25
	0	25

Figure 1. Example of a Social Selling Index (SSI)

SSI GOAL #2: Be above your industry average.
Your target is: _____

Make it your goal to get to and maintain a minimum SSI of 60. If you're in sales, it should be well over 80. Scores between two and four are surprisingly common, and I have seen SSI ratings of zero. (I don't know how one can even *have* a LinkedIn profile and be at zero, but trust me, it's possible!)

Don't worry where you are right now; just work to get it well over 60 as quickly as you can. Following the advice in this book will help you make a huge leap, so commit to getting your SSI score up and then keep it high, through consistent participation across the four areas it measures.

SSI GOAL 1: _____

by what date ____/_____/20___

Your SSI measures four key ways in which you can use LinkedIn to achieve professional success:

1. Establish your professional brand (which we'll discuss below);

2. Find the right people;

3. Engage with insights; and

4. Build relationships.

When building your presence on LinkedIn, these four areas are great places to focus your energy to ensure you are building a strong brand the right way. When you go to the SSI page, each of these categories has an explanatory PowerPoint attached, so you can learn more about how to get strong in all four categories.

Establish Your Professional Brand

The essential first step to creating an all-star LinkedIn profile is easy: fill in your profile as completely as possible and keep it updated. If you do everything I suggest here, you can expect your SSI to skyrocket after completing just these steps.

I work with multinationals, ranging from tech companies to banks, where the vast majority of professionals are within the SSI range of 20 to 40. Multinationals are really starting to focus on employee advocacy, with particular emphasis on LinkedIn. Being a social leader as a business professional—no matter your role in your organization—will be critical for your future. It will be expected. So, get ahead of the curve and start raising your SSI score to a minimum of 60.

The next three steps require more consistent effort.

Find the Right
People

Here is a chance to address an often-asked question: *should I connect on LinkedIn with people I haven't met before?* And my answer is yes. In the old days of LinkedIn, we were encouraged to only connect with people we had met in real life. However, to become a powerful social leader, you need to network with professionals outside your first-degree connections. That's one reason to do it.

Now, there will always be people you connect with who spam you immediately. Fortunately, it has never been easier to *unfollow* someone on LinkedIn. If you're a woman, you may also get men connecting to tell you how beautiful you are and asking if you are open to having a relationship. It's not Tinder, but some people missed that message. There are also bots on LinkedIn.

My advice is to be selective. Establish rules—such as, *only connect with people who have 10 or more connections in common with you*—and follow them. Make it 50 connections if you want to be sure. However, to become a social leader, your goal should be to connect with your entire industry and to get beyond your immediate network, because that is how you become powerful on social media. You may not have personally met everyone face-to-face yet, but you can start building relationships across your industry with LinkedIn today.

With this in mind, I encourage you to connect with people you have not met before in person, but who are aligned with your career. Who knows which of them may be a future employer or employee, or someone who will learn from you and promote your work? The stranger who sends you a request may have heard you speak and been inspired by your words. You won't know if you don't connect.

Twitter used to be the only platform that gave you a global audience well beyond your direct network. It provided a platform to connect with the international thought-leaders in your field. Today, if you intelligently build your network on LinkedIn, you can grow a powerful community interested in what you have to say. Connect with everyone you know, but make sure you stay open to other great connection opportunities.

My rules for connecting with people are:

(Draft them, you can refine over time)

1. _____

   _____

2. _____

   _____

3. _____

   _____

Engage With
Insights and Build
Relationships

Engaging or actively participating is what really matters when building a powerful social leadership presence—and increasing your SSI score over the long haul. Talk to people. Comment on what others are sharing. Tag people in the content you share (simply put @ and then type their name).

Contrary to the way many people use it, LinkedIn is not a megaphone for your views and ideas. It's not a platform to tell people what you're doing and how successful you are at it. Most participants on LinkedIn don't mind a little bit of self-promotion, but if that's all you do, you're missing the *real* opportunity.

LinkedIn is a platform to build relationships and a community.

You can't do this if you're treating it as a one-way street. Build a real community. Support people you admire and get involved in conversations. Comment on posts. Share great content. Participate. Encourage. This is what LinkedIn is really all about.

The SSI measurement categories, far from being meaningless statistics, assess how you align with LinkedIn's core values: connecting, engaging, adding value, and building a powerful tribe.

How Do You
Compare with Your
Peers?

Look at your network average to find out. This useful SSI metric, found by scrolling down on your SSI page, shows you the average score in *your* network/industry. Make it a goal to consistently exceed this average. SSI averages can vary wildly between industries. My network's average is relatively high, for example, because I'm connected to a lot of people like me. However, in the marketing/advertising industry the average sits at around 26, a figure I find surprising. Leaders in this industry in particular should have mastery of all platforms, given that you can only really understand social media if you participate fully in it.

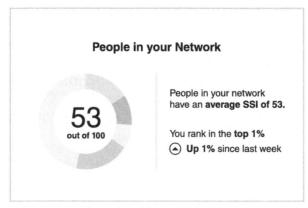

Figure 2. Example of an Average SSI

Equally amazing is that social selling skills continue to be abysmally low across all industries, with estimates suggesting only 15 percent of people in sales are socially selling. The SSI index is likely to become a job criteria and recruitment factor for sales professionals soon. Why? Because internal research at large global companies back the claim that leaders with higher SSI scores get better sales results. **If you're in sales or business development, it's time to take SSI very, very seriously.**

And you need to do this now—*before* your company sets a minimum SSI requirement for your role! I struggle to understand why professionals will only act when they are required to by their company. The personal career benefits of being a social leader should be enough of an incentive.

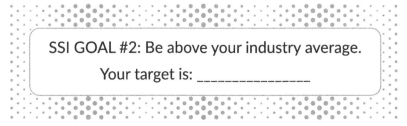

SSI GOAL #2: Be above your industry average.

Your target is: _____

Stay ahead of the curve on SSI requirements. Get on board and own your voice.

When you enter editing mode on your profile, ensure the **share with network button** is turned **OFF**.

Figure 3. Turn off share with network

This is what you'll see when you click on *edit profile* (scroll down if you can't see it). The on/off toggle has moved from its original place in the right-hand column, so keep an eye out for it at the bottom of the menu. It will be grey when off and a brighter blue when on. Just make sure you slide the toggle to **off** for basic updates and turn it back on for significant changes in your career.

It's great to alert your network when you are starting a new position, or once in a while when something significant happens, but you don't want everyone in your network getting a notification every time you tweak your profile.

I once forgot to turn this toggle off when changing my role from Asia-Pacific to Asia. Before I knew it, I had 100 congratulatory messages on the new job that wasn't new. Face palm! I also forgot to turn it ON when I launched The Digital Conversationalist, which was a big missed opportunity to raise awareness on my new brand!

Why These 18 Steps, Why Now?

For half a decade, I've run my social leadership course with professionals working for the world's largest companies. I love this work. This content remains relevant.

Professionals were at zero when it came to where to start on LinkedIn, and so I put together these critical steps to ensure attendees had the basics in hand to get their LinkedIn presence up to date and looking great, along with some critical guidance on what matters from the outset.

It's important to get this part of the process done and dusted before moving on to the next phase—building a powerful presence around meaningful intention. These 18 steps will provide the guidance you need to get the basics down and get your career and your business moving.

1 SET UP
YOUR PROFILE PROPERLY

If you don't already have a LinkedIn profile, it's time to set one up. If you do have one, make sure you fill in all of the sections relevant to you. Here is the basic information you need to get started.

To check the contact information you have already, click on your profile, and below your banner, you will see these four points. Click on *see contact info* and make sure you've included all the information you want to have available for your contacts.

- ❑ **Name**

- ❑ **Professional title**: We'll talk about this in more detail later. Just let your current role be your professional title for now, and it will be populated automatically if you don't write an original one.

- ❑ **Previous positions**: Fill in as much information as you can. If you have big gaps that's ok, but you should explain them so readers aren't left to their own imagination. For example, you can list travel or parenting duties to explain gaps in your work history.

❏ **Education**: Fill it in as far back as you want to go, but I don't recommend including high school unless you are still in high school or have recently graduated.

❏ **Email**: You must provide an email address for your LinkedIn profile, but remember, it's visible to anyone you connect with. I recommend using a personal email, versus a company email, as you never know when you will move on. However, if your company pays for LinkedIn Navigator or other LinkedIn services, you may need to use your company address while in their employment.

❏ **Instant messenger, phone number, and address:** Add these if you want to. But remember, they are visible to connections. I don't include my phone number or address.

❏ **Twitter handle**: What's a handle? It's your address on Twitter or Instagram. My handle, for example, is @AndreaTEdwards. If you don't have one yet, remember to go back to LinkedIn and update it later. Your Twitter handle is critical if you blog on LinkedIn; it automatically includes your handle in tweets when other people share your blogs from LinkedIn.

❑ **Website**: Do you have a website or a blog? You can also include the website of a company you work for.

❑ **Set to public profile**: Please, make sure your profile is public. There are virtually no reasons to have an anonymous profile on LinkedIn.

❑ *Tick when completed!*

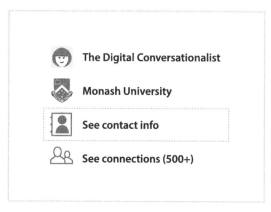

Figure 4. Where to find contact info

Edit Your Public Profile

This view is on the right-hand column of the *edit public profile* page. My advice is to set your profile as public, unless you have a very good reason for being anonymous or private.

Fill in as much detail as you can on your LinkedIn profile and remember to keep this updated as additional information becomes relevant. However, do be thoughtful about what you include, as all of this information can be seen by your connections.

To illustrate: I am focused on building a big community to get more exposure for my blogs, so I am generous about who I connect with. The problem with this approach is that when we share a lot of information, we make this information accessible to all new connections, which is probably how I end up on so many email marketing lists, that curse of the digital age! I am definitely more practiced at unsubscribing and blocking contacts than I used to be.

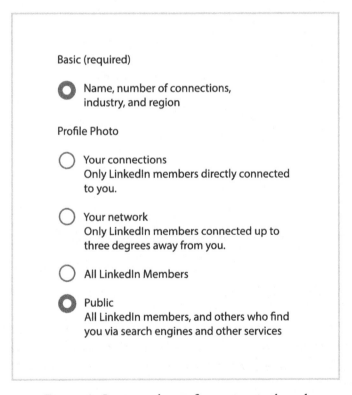

Figure 5. Setting what information is shared

This is also why I don't share my phone number or address. Email, I can cope with. More phone calls or junk mail by post—not so much.

If your goal is to become an influencer, you must go beyond your immediate community to grow your reach and impact. Even if you don't want to *go big*, how often do you meet recruiters or potential employers online before you meet face-to-face? LinkedIn isn't Facebook, and you're here precisely because you want the right kind of exposure, *not* anonymity.

You can create a unique address for your LinkedIn profile, and this is a great opportunity to personalize your presence.

Why is this important? A personalized address makes it easier to promote and share your profile at events and on your email signature, your business cards, and your blog. When you share your Twitter handle or other social media assets, make sure you are maximizing your LinkedIn address as well.

Edit public profile URL

Enhance your personal brand by creating a custom URL for your LinkedIn public profile.

www.linkedin.com/andreatedwards ✏

Figure 6. Editing your url

Updating your address is a simple process. Simply go to the *edit public profile* page, and in the top right column you'll see the option to edit your public profile URL. Click on the pencil icon to get rid of the numbers and dashes in your name.

Hint—Create a Consistent Professional Social Media Presence

If you have a consistent professional brand name across social media platforms, you'll be easier to find and your promotion will be more effective. My handle, no matter the platform, is @AndreaTEdwards. If you are late doing this and someone else nabbed your name, you may need to be creative. Those with very common names often miss out on having their own names on their LinkedIn profile. If you have a Twitter profile already, I suggest using the same name. Either way, decide what is the right professional name for yourself on social media and then use it everywhere.

Once you've done this, remember to promote your social media name and link to your profiles in all the right places: as a permanent part of your email signature, in presentations, at the end of blogs, and on business cards.

❑ **I've updated my LinkedIn web address to be my name (or close to it)**

This is What You Look Like Without a Photo

Figure 7. Faceless without photo

Not having a photo on social media is unacceptable. If you have no photo and you try to connect with anyone who takes real people and social media seriously, your request will often be rejected immediately. A profile without a photo effectively sends the following messages with your request:

You don't take social media seriously.

You have absolutely no idea what you are doing and don't deserve to be taken seriously.

You are a bot or spam account, and none of us want to connect with these if we can avoid it.

Adding a photo means it's 14 times more likely your profile will be found and visited, and you are 36 times more likely to receive a message from a contact.

Update Your Profile Picture

Your photo needs to be relatively professional. It's not going to be a photo of you sitting in your mum's kitchen or at a party with your mates, it's going to have a simple background, and it's going to look great. If you don't have a photo, get your camera out and ask someone to take a picture of you in front of a wall. Aim for something plain, though color or texture can nicely compliment your headshot.

A gentle suggestion: ask your photographer to stand above you to avoid a double chin. #justsayin.

Specifications for Your Profile Photo

You can upload JPG, GIF, or PNG files.

File size is 8MB maximum.

Your photo should be square.

The ideal pixel size for your photo is 400 x 400 or 7680 (W) by 4320 (H) pixels.

If either width or height exceeds 20,000 pixels, your photo will not upload.

For the most current information on photo size or any other details on LinkedIn, the best resource is LinkedIn help.[5]

Once you have taken your photo, some careful photo editing can make for a brighter, more flattering headshot— it's amazing how many years you can take off! However, go easy with the editing tools—if you doctor your photo too much not only will it be obvious, but people might not recognize you when they meet you face-to-face.

It's important to crop the photo as close to your face as you can. This ensures a good headshot, not a tiny head with a big, distracting background. This is more important than ever, given that most people will view your image on their phone. Check how your profile looks on your phone. Can you see your face?

Select a Banner Picture

The banner is the rectangular blue space above your profile photo on LinkedIn. A good banner can make your profile pop, and it's an important opportunity for visual storytelling.

Sixty-three percent of the world's population are visual learners. What kind of visual story should your banner tell? People choose lots of things, from corporate branding or themselves speaking onstage to suggestive imagery like city skylines, golf courses, green spaces, and oceans. Another option I recommend is colors and textures.

I change my banner often – in fact, it will probably feature this book if you check my profile today - and it's currently a photo of a book I recently co-launched - Unleash Your Voice: Powerful Public Speaking for Every

---

5.   https://www.linkedin.com/help

Woman.[6] Before I had things like books to share, my most frequent default banners were always "red bling," because red is my favorite color and the bling makes me happy when I look at it. I've used red sparkly hearts and red "dragon skin." Don't forget to keep changing your banner, because nothing should be stagnant in the digital world.

I often use my own photography, but I'm also prepared to spend money on visual assets. At a bare minimum, you should search for free stock photography and look for a color, texture, or idea that aligns with your personal theme. Shutterstock[7] is my stock photo library of choice, and while today I pay for the service, I would like to give them a shout-out here to thank them for making me one of their influencers for a couple of years. I love the site and the amazing quality of photos and images there.

A key benefit of Shutterstock is their editing tool, which lets you upload images and customize them be to the right size for all social media channels—all in the one place. You can also add information, directly to your photos, including social media handles and website information. If you don't want to outsource or you don't have the budget, using the tools available on the professional stock photo sites is a possibility.

Please remember that the most important money you will spend, if you take social media and blogging seriously, is on your imagery. It's critical if you want to gain traction and attention. The tools available online make it very easy for all of us to look professional on social media. In addition to the editing tools I mentioned above, the app

---

6. https://www.amazon.com/Unleash-Your-Voice-Powerful-Speaking/dp/154374995X
7. https://www.shutterstock.com

Canva,[8] among others, provides an array of free graphic-design tools.

If you have a social media budget, I recommend going to sites like Fiverr.com and Upwork.com, where you can find a very affordable designer to create a personal banner that you can use on LinkedIn and any other sites or platforms you use for professional communication. Recent changes to the LinkedIn layout give you more space to work with than ever before, so definitely invest as much as you can in how you use it.

Linkedin Banner Specifications

The dimensions for the banner are minimum 1584 (w) x 396 (h) pixels

The file needs to be JPG, PNG, or GIF

Maximum 8MB

I recommend that your banner be something meaningful to you. To ensure you are not breaking any copyright laws, best practice is to either buy your image or take the photo or design the image yourself.

Here are three CEOs I like. Check out their current look on LinkedIn—including photo and banner:

Sir Richard Branson[9]

Jeff Weiner,[10] CEO of LinkedIn

Arianna Huffington[11]

---

8.   https://www.canva.com/
9.   https://www.linkedin.com/in/rbranson/
10. https://www.linkedin.com/in/jeffweiner08/
11. https://www.linkedin.com/in/ariannahuffington/

The bottom line is that anyone who takes LinkedIn seriously views a profile without a banner image as an incomplete job. It tells us that this person does not understand the power of LinkedIn. It's a small but important detail in having a complete profile. It's also a piece of digital real estate many people fail to maximize. Appeal to the visual learners amongst us—and look great too.

❑ **I've updated my photo**: Make it a nice photo, it's representing you.

❑ **I've updated my banner:** Do something that is meaningful to you, that visually shows who you are professionally.

4 WRITE YOUR PROFESSIONAL HEADLINE

This might seem like a very small detail, but you should plan to spend a decent amount of time on this line, which is more important than meets the eye. Your current role automatically populates this space, so as long as you have indicated a current role there will be information here already. The first three things people see on LinkedIn are your photo, your name, and your professional headline.

Figure 8. Your headline with photo and banner

Your headline is the text that follows your name. In the example above the headline is *Helping businesses and professionals tell better stories, while rousing passion in people to embrace social leadership.*

Think of your headline as the place where you make your first impression.

When Do Your Connections See Your Headline?

When they search for your name they see it, as it's now part of the search text.

When you write a comment, they see it.

When you send an invitation, they see it.

When you participate in groups, they see it.

When they click on your profile, they see it.

When they read a blog you post, they see it.

It's Critical. So, What Should it Say?

I always recommend having a look at the kinds of headlines other people in your field are using. That being said, don't be afraid to be different—or a first in your industry. I often encourage very senior executives to use their job title, since they are senior enough that it's appropriate. However there are many more ways to approach writing a headline.

Here are examples of some titles from my contacts on LinkedIn—no preference or order.

Wendy (Hogan) McEwan—*Connecting people and property*

Lindley Craig—*Building better individuals who build better companies*

Stacey Albert—*Leading digital cloud transformations across the globe!*

Drew Calin—*Helping companies mobilise across Asia*

Joanne FLINN—the Business Growth Lady – *Innovation | Human Performance | Capital Raising*

Natasha David—*Helping B2B champions find their voices and tell their stories*

Olivier Legrand—*Creating economic opportunities for professionals and entrepreneurs in Asia with the incredible LinkedIn Asia Team*

Tiffani Bova—*Anthropologist of Growth Companies | Storyteller | Innovation Evangelist at Salesforce | WSJ Bestselling Author*

Gina Romero—*Matching entrepreneurs, speakers and small business owners with talented Executive Virtual Assistants*

Stephanie Dickson—*Founder Green Is The New Black | Conscious Community Builder | Event Organiser | Speaker*

Darren Keppie—*Unlocking the Power of Employee Advocacy for the World's Leading Brands*

What Should Your Headline Be?

Which of these examples stood out to you? Perhaps you didn't like any of them. Would you prefer to feature your job title instead? There is no one answer, and I shared this collection to give you an idea of the variety of headlines professionals use for their LinkedIn profiles.

One approach when defining your title is to answer the question: *who do you help?* Audience focus is everything today, but if you take a look, most LinkedIn Headlines are not audience focused at all.

So, can you fill in the dots?

"I help professionals..."

"I help businesses..."

Try on the following words: I *enable, empower, facilitate, inspire, encourage, galvanize, rouse, energize, support, unlock, build,* and so on. **An excellent thesaurus is a gift during this process.**

The important lesson is that in today's digital world, all content you create (including your social media profiles) should be focused on your audience, and this is your foremost opportunity to talk to *your* audience and tell them how *you* can help them.

As you may have noticed, many of the examples I provided above are from fairly creative fields or roles. That's because my community is a predominantly creative one, but that might not suit you. If none of these examples speak to you, I recommend you look through *your* connections' professional headlines and take inspiration there.

Another very important strategy is to focus on **key words relevant to your job**, because LinkedIn is a search engine, and Google loves LinkedIn too. My title is full of key words for my field. What are the key words for yours?

> **Sales:** sales, sales leadership, CRM, social selling expert
> **Marketing:** customer experience, big data, content marketing, social media, growth hacker
> **Leadership:** management, innovation, transformational leader, building talent

You may have noticed some professionals using the vertical line symbol— | —rather than commas between words or phrases in their LinkedIn title. Stars also make an appearance on LinkedIn today, as do ticks and other images, but is it your style? It's not mine, which is why I don't use images or symbols in my headline. Do what feels right for you. These visual elements certainly help if you want to stand out a little more.

If you are a senior leader in business, the common practice is to use your title. The higher up you are, the more sense this makes. However, consider using your title *and* making it personal by writing a mini-statement at the end to embody who you are.

Two Examples

—making a difference...

—a transformational leader with passion

You may have noticed that I give **Andrea T Edwards, CSP—The Digital Conversationalist** as my name. When I established my company, I decided that my name and brand needed to be synonymous, which is why **The Digital Conversationalist** is included with my name on my profile. You can do this too.

I have to admit though, that this wasn't an easy thing for me to do. I naturally avoid anything that feels like arrogance or flamboyance, so it felt like a big step. I thought long and hard about it, realizing that if I wanted to stand out in my field, then I had to buckle down and own what makes me stand out. Should you? If you're an entrepreneur or thought-leader, why not?

However, if you are an employee, is it appropriate? Only you can answer this question. Whatever you do, please don't be afraid to have your own style. On the other hand, don't do something you're not comfortable with.

And remember, you have 120 characters to use (including spaces) AND if you don't write a professional headline in your own style, your current job title will automatically be used. That is fine too, but why not use the space to make an impact and let your audience know you better?

I encourage you to be bold, if it feels right. Stand out. Be brave. And be you.

Draft your headline. Try several, it may take some exploration to develop. If you have marketing friends, ask them to help you.

_____

_____

_____

_____

❑ **My headline reflects me**: Be appropriate, be bold and be authentically yourself.

5 TIME TO
WRITE YOUR SUMMARY

Now it's time to focus on your professional summary, and this is **really** important. A little exploring of profiles from your industry will show you that there are many different approaches to writing this piece. There is no right or wrong way; what matters is tell your story and feel good about it. In this section I'll outline what *I* believe makes an effective summary.

Write it in the **first person**. That may feel uncomfortable for you, as it does for many people, but it comes across as more genuine in first person. To overcome any qualms, write it in the third person, and once you're happy with it, flip it into the first person. This will give you permission to be bold.

What to write? It's a snapshot of your professional career, what you do, and what you focus on. Remember to include keywords relevant to your industry. LinkedIn will encourage you to do this, but as an example, if you are in sales, include terms such as *sales*, *sales leadership* or *customer service*. This is how you will be found when professionals are searching LinkedIn for people like *you*.

But don't just write about your work. Write about your values, what you care about, what you stand for—

and please, don't be afraid to use humor, especially if you are naturally a funny person. This is about you, the person, because you're not a machine. It's important to write this section in a way that will engage readers. There are enough boring summaries out there—why stay in that herd?

Also, resist the temptation to make this section read like a resume or CV. That information should be available in your position descriptions throughout the rest of your LinkedIn profile, so try not to double up on what you have already said. Tell people a story. Let them get to know you and the type of person you are. Do you care about women's issues? Talk about your engagement there. Is employee engagement close to your heart? Tell us why and how. Are you passionate about technology and its potential to change the world? Great—share that passion.

I also advise that you **do not** use bullet points to highlight your achievements in your summary. Visually, bullets don't look good on LinkedIn anyway, as it's not a platform designed for dots. Furthermore, there is plenty of real estate on LinkedIn to list your achievements—in your position descriptions and awards sections, for example. Use your summary to get people excited about the person that you are.

As a visual supplement to your summary (and for your roles as well) LinkedIn offers great possibilities to tell your story using photos, weblinks, YouTube videos, SlideShares, PDFs, and more. Visual storytelling is easy to do, offers your audience the chance to go deeper into your background, and rounds out your profile to be more engaging on multiple levels. Maximize this opportunity.

Here are some suggestions on where you can find content to feature in your summary (and positions). If you don't already do so, make it a point to capture your professional moments from this day forward.

> Media coverage
> SlideShare decks
> LinkedIn blog posts
> Your blog posts
> Guest blog posts
> YouTube videos
> Your work
> Photos at work
> Event photos
> Company photos
> Company off-site activities
> Team activities
> Speaking onstage

And as with all aspects of your LinkedIn profile, keep updating your summary with fresh images and new directions or achievements in your story.

Finding great LinkedIn profile examples is surprisingly difficult. I have done a lot of research to find the best people with the most compelling summaries on the platform. During my search, I found a list of the Fortune 500 Chief Marketing Officers and I figured if anyone could get it right, surely the best marketing professionals in the world would, right?

Unfortunately, not even the best of the Fortune 500 CMOs were fantastic, in my opinion. And what about LinkedIn's most searched profiles or Power Profiles? Well, it seems that while people may be *looking* for these people, very few of those "Power Profiles" are actually embracing all the powerful features that LinkedIn offers—as evidenced by their incomplete profiles.

I see so many missed opportunities on LinkedIn, and often it comes down to the basic stuff, such as not writing a compelling summary, having a poor-quality profile photo, or not telling a visual story. The good news is that if you complete your profile in an engaging and intelligent way, you'll automatically have a better LinkedIn profile than most people out there!

Here are profiles by some executives who, I believe, are getting it right:

Stanimira Koleva[12]

Eric Schnatterly[13]

Tiffani Bova[14]

Wendy (Hogan) McEwan[15]

There are many great examples where you can find inspiration. But your job, once you've learned all you can from other people's profiles, is to decide on a style that suits you.

What Makes a Poor Summary?

Summaries written in the third person. I strongly suggest using the first person if you want to tell a genuine story and reach people's hearts and minds.

---

12. https://www.linkedin.com/in/stanimirakoleva/
13. https://www.linkedin.com/in/ericschnatterly/
14. https://www.linkedin.com/in/tiffanibova/
15. https://www.linkedin.com/in/wendyhogan/

Writing summaries as a career overview. We can look through your LinkedIn profile for that—tell us something we don't know.

Failing to tell a visual story at all—don't miss this important opportunity!

Failing to tell a story that helps the world understand what sort of a person you are. We are bringing the whole person to the table, so be authentic and real in your summary.

The following fill-in-the-blank sentences will help you create a great and meaningful summary:

> I have been in...
> Throughout my career I have valued/focused on...
> I care about...
> ...is important to me.
> I have lived and worked in...
> ...has taught me....

Make writing an effective summary a priority. It's natural to feel daunted by this, because we are not all born storytellers and writing about ourselves can feel like self-promotion. Ask for help if you need it, but do the work yourself. Tell your own story. If you completely outsource this piece, I guarantee it won't come across as authentic.

If you can make it a priority to write your summary, it will help you be successful in completing and being proud of your profile. **Don't get stuck here**, as people often do. Just get it done. On the other hand, if you just can't do it, don't let it hold you back from participating on LinkedIn. Move on until you feel comfortable writing an engaging summary about yourself.

Notes—List my key words, statements, and points I want to make as a leader in my field.

_____

_____

_____

_____

❏ **I've updated my summary**: It's in first person and I'm happy to have it read. It shows me as a full, well-rounded career person.

6 COVER YOUR HISTORY, UPDATE YOUR POSITIONS

The older you are, the longer this is going to take, but it's critical to make sure your entire career history is up to date. If you have an old resumé, print it out as a reference to use while you fill in your LinkedIn profile.

Keep in mind that even in this section, you can give yourself permission to not be boring. The further back you go, the less you will feel inclined to add information, but include as much as you can, even if it is just the job title, company, and employment dates. Talk about achievements, what you loved about the job, and maybe even why you moved on—if it's positive. You can tell a wonderful story across your career-span.

If you have career gaps, don't be afraid to explain them, for gaps are becoming more and more accepted in the business world today, especially for the younger generation, who are changing roles faster than ever before. Long-term travel, parenting, sabbaticals, time off for education and other reasons for career breaks are not things to hide. Trust in the human truth that the right employers will value your life experience.

Once you have entered all your text content, the next step is reviewing the way you use visual elements. I recommend adding photos, links, SlideShare decks, or

YouTube videos for every role that you list. If you don't have relevant images for past roles, add some inspirational messages.

Try and use images that mean something to you or show you participating in something, and also remember to include images of the company in question for present and past roles. The images don't have to be of you—but keep in mind that this is about celebrating your career, so don't be shy. And please, don't let these images be static. Keep updating them and shuffling the order, especially in your current position and summary.

Here's what you currently see under my summary— but not for long, because I update it regularly!

Figure 9. Images with summary

And this is under my current role...

Figure 10. Images with current job

...all the way back to my first job as a musician in the Australian Army.

Figure 11. Images with very first job

See, I'm telling a story here. People are curious to meet the gal who served in the military early in her career, and as a professional musician to boot! What's unique, intriguing, and worth sharing as part of your story?

❑ **I've added my career history**, including the interesting other things I may have done over the years.

7 FOLLOW
COMPANIES, THE MEDIA, AND INFLUENCERS

Recruitment remains a core part of LinkedIn, but its primary focus is as a content platform, and as such, it's only as powerful an influence as *you* let it be. I've said it before: when you get to the point where you are checking LinkedIn on the weekend the way you would Instagram or Facebook, you'll know that you've upped your LinkedIn game to make it a rich and valuable platform for yourself, personally and professionally.

The best way to bring LinkedIn's phenomenal power as a content platform into your life and news feed is by following great people and businesses. You can follow influencers, companies, news sources, and, of course, the best people you know. Doing so will make your LinkedIn news feed a rich information platform, which means you'll visit and engage with it every day.

When people complain that their LinkedIn feed is full of nonsense, I want to say to them, it's only as good as who you follow. If it's full of nonsense, unfollow those who do not inspire you and focus on following the best there is.

Start With Influencers

I'm going to talk about the increasing importance of hashtags later on, but as a starting point, LinkedIn influencers are worth following.

There are 500 official **LinkedIn influencers**, including high-level business leaders, public figures (such as presidents and prime ministers), authors, celebrities, and speakers. In today's world anyone can become an influencer, but following your favorite LinkedIn influencers is a great way to fill your news feed with awesome content—and it's shareable content too.

Figure 12. LinkedIn influencers

Companies

You should also follow **companies**: the one you work for, companies you admire, and companies that are delivering world-class business information relevant to you. McKinsey, for example, remains my favorite business information source. If you have strategic customers or partners, you should follow them too. And what about companies that just fascinate you? For example, I follow Disney. How cool is Disney? What companies intrigue you or strike your fancy?

If you're on the job hunt, following the companies you want to work for should be a no-brainer, as well as reviewing their LinkedIn company pages before an interview. With that said, many companies aren't doing a great job with content on their company pages because they still see LinkedIn as nothing more than a recruitment platform. The content landscape is improving as corporates slowly realize LinkedIn is about delivering empowering information that helps customers, not just talking about how great your business is.

I recommend checking out your own company page (follow it!) and see what you think; is it compelling enough to entice you to learn from it every day? That should be your company goal. If it's full of business achievements and awards your company has won, it is not delivering anything meaningful to customers and it won't draw people in every day.

Company pages are only valuable when they bring actual value to audience. If you have any role in creating or maintaining your organization's LinkedIn company page, remember it is a place to deliver value to your audience. It's not a soap box for your business, which is how too many companies continue to use it.

News Sources

This used to be a different section on LinkedIn, with many specific topics to follow, but now topics have moved under hashtags—which makes sense! However, most global news channels are available on LinkedIn, so following them is a great way to keep up to date with news and views relevant to your field and expertise. Whatever your news habits, following the most compelling sites will ensure that your LinkedIn feed is rich with information that is relevant and helpful to you.

I've followed:

(cross off when completed)

❑ My company on LinkedIn

❑ Companies I admire, companies I want to work for, businesses I work with today

❑ A selection of the Top 500 Influencers

❑ Peers I admire, my friends and former colleagues

❑ Topics I am interested in

❑ The media I track

8 USE HASHTAGS

Hashtags, once the cryptic language of Twitter, are hugely relevant today across Facebook, Twitter, Pinterest, Instagram, YouTube, SnapChat, Tik Tok and, since August 2016, LinkedIn and SlideShare.[16] Introducing hashtags and subsequently increasing their importance on the platform has made LinkedIn an even more powerful social force in the corporate world. Hashtags link you to everyone else using a particular hashtag, allowing you to join a global conversation on your topic of expertise. It's how you get and keep people's attention and how you elevate your brand and voice to be heard beyond your immediate community.

Unless you use hashtags, you are basically invisible to anyone who is not directly connected to you. Far from being teen slang or for significant events only, hashtags are a critical factor in building a bigger profile and a strong personal brand.

Hashtags link you to the people and ideas you care about most—and to the people searching for information on the topics you speak out on. It's how you build your profile beyond your immediate

---

16.   https://blog.linkedin.com/2016/08/25/tap-into-professional-knowledge-with-content-search-at-linkedin

network. It's how you get aligned to and establish yourself as an expert on the topics you care about, digitally. If you want to be a powerhouse on social media, hashtags are essential.

Hashtags are relevant to global and topical conversations (or #moments), but they are also relevant to industries, job titles, and core topics of expertise.

A few examples across some core topics:

Figure 13. Hashtag examples

To become known as an expert in your field, use hashtags relevant to core topics in your field, especially if you want to grow your profile beyond your immediate community.

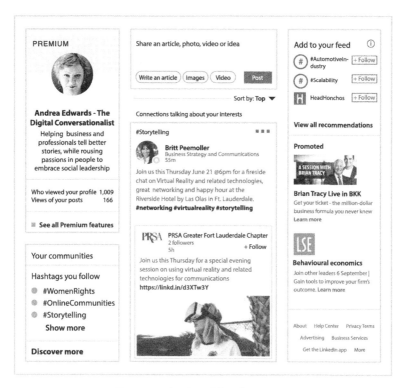

Figure 14. Good hashtagging

In this screenshot from my news feed, you'll see that my connection Britt Peemoller has included the hashtag #storytelling in a post she made. Because LinkedIn knows I'm interested in storytelling, it has flagged her post in my feed, bringing my attention directly to it as something relevant to me. I like it!

Having your feed populated and focused on the topics you care about is AWESOME and ensures that LinkedIn will continue to be a powerhouse content platform.

Another thing you should notice in the image above is on the bottom left. You'll see **Your Communities** and below that, hashtags you follow.

Figure 15. List of hastags on LinkedIn

To follow hashtags on LinkedIn, all you have to do is click on **Discover More**. See all the hashtags you can follow? Go through this vast list and follow the ones that are most meaningful to you. Don't forget to pay attention to the numbers of followers, too.

This is *really* how you bring LinkedIn—as a content and connections platform—to life for yourself. If you use hashtags well, you can easily open your profile up to third-degree connections, who will see you featured in their news feeds based on your hashtag use.

This brilliant evolution toward hashtags will tackle so many of the challenges LinkedIn is facing, from a noisy nonsense-content perspective. But for all of us, it means we must get into the habit of using hashtags and using them intelligently—everywhere, but especially on LinkedIn.

Which Hashtags Should You Follow?

What hashtags are the thought leaders in your field using? LinkedIn might not be the best place to discover this, since so many people there are still not using them, so check other social platforms too.

What are the common company hashtags you could be using to tie yourself into a bigger global conversation?

Twitter and Instagram are great sites to search for hashtags, even if you don't have an account. Instagram allows you to see how popular a hashtag is by tracking the number of times it has been used. At the time of this writing, #PhotoOfTheDay is the most popular hashtag in the world.

Use the sites hashtags.org, top-hashtags.com, and hashtagify.com as reference points in your research.

An example of a big name in my field is Jeff Bullas.[17] He hashtags his posts with #Marketing #Blogging #DigitalMarketing #SocialMedia #Events #Digital #BloggingTips #Wordpress. Given his status as the top social media expert in the world, I figure that if he uses these hashtags, they'll work for me, too! Who is your Jeff Bullas?

Remember, no one owns hashtags and the possibilities are endless. You don't need to use one that already exists— start a trend. However, using well established hashtags is a good way to elevate your visibility in your field.

How Hashtags are being used on LinkedIn: the Good, the Bad, and the Terrible

Using hashtags is a new practice for many active LinkedIn users. And if you've been using them elsewhere, don't make the mistake of using hashtags on LinkedIn the same way you do on other platforms. It's important to understand how to harness and tailor their power specifically for LinkedIn, though the practices I'll discuss below are relevant across other platforms too.

> https://lnkd.in/fBsYn_S #centralbanks #financial #crisis #globalization #geopolitics

Figure 16. Poor hashtagging

Using hashtags as the only content in your comment delivers no value to your audience, even if it gets you into a healthy spot in LinkedIn's back-end. Please, never

---

17. https://Twitter.com/jeffbullas

miss an opportunity to bring something meaningful to your audience. Remember, it's about them, not you. Tell people *why* you're sharing information and finish with hashtags. How many hashtags to use? No more than three. On Instagram up to ten is standard, but elsewhere and especially on LinkedIn, limit your hashtags to three.

😂 ✌ #lol ✈

#travel #holidays #vacation sooner **#pensionfunds @passiveincome #retirementsavings #financialfreedom** earlier. **#independence #networkmarketing #leisuretravel #leisureindustry #disruptivetechnologies #travelphotography #traveltechnology #travelmarketing #travelblogging #travelplanning #wordofmouthmarketing @wordofmouth #socialmediamarketing #socialmedia #entrepreneurship #teamspirit #homebasedbusiness**

Figure 17. Worse hashtagging

This beauty of an example (and please note, dear reader, that in Australia, "beauty" is not necessarily a complement), is what I call an Instagram post, and it has no place on LinkedIn. Where is the actual text in this post? If you look carefully, there are only two non-hashtag words: *sooner* and *earlier*. The rest requires a lot of effort to read, and it certainly doesn't make sense, editorially. You don't want to make anything hard to read or unclear on social media, so keep hashtags separate from the content and put them—sparingly—at the end of your post.

Example three: well done, Olive! (PS Olive is an awesome lady)

Olive Huang
Research Vice President at Gartner
1h

What a fun packed event! Thank you all for spending the past two days with us at the Gartner Customer Experience and Technologies summit in Sydney.
#customerexperience #gartnercs Tatiana Wells Ed Thompson Ben Zelos Susan Moore

Figure 18. Great hashtagging

Take a good look at hashtags done right in an effective post. Concisely say what you want to say, add the relevant hashtags, copy the relevant people, and—look at that: we have a winner, not only in my books but based on lots of experience and research across social media. Take note of what works in posts you like, but it's ultimately up to you to decide how you will approach using hashtags.

The ongoing evolution in hashtag use on LinkedIn puts the information you're interested in at the forefront of what the platform is all about, so:

- Work out what hashtags you should be using.

- Follow hashtags on topics that are important to you.

- Use hashtags to get your content in front of new and relevant audiences.

- Build a hashtag habit.

- Put them at the end of your comments, but don't overdo your use of hashtags.

And finally, try not to be overwhelmed by hashtags, if you haven't yet acquired the habit. Trust me, it doesn't take much effort to turn yourself into a hashtag champion. Simply click on **Discover More**, which is at the bottom left when you open LinkedIn. If you can't see it, this means you haven't been using hashtags. To get this option to appear, share something awesome and finish your post with a couple of hashtags relevant to your business or industry (get ideas from the image above if you like).

Once you land on the **Discover More** page, you'll be able to see the topics people currently care most about on LinkedIn and you can follow the ones that interest you. After that, all you need to do is start using them!

Hashtags empower you to be present in global conversations and they allow people to find you. This means they can engage with you, follow you, or track you, opening up your opportunity to become a valuable leader to them, and influence the conversations that define your field.

Some additional hashtag guidance:

- Use one hashtag consistently if you work for a company. If you work for IBM use #IBM and two others.

- If you want to be a thought leader in a particular sector, use common hashtags for that sector, such as #FSI #Insurance #Biotech #Healthcare or #Aerospace.

- If you're in a specific role, like marketing, use the most relevant hashtags: #Marketing #CMO #DigitalMarketing #CX #BigData #Analytics #SocialMedia #Advertising or #Branding.

- If you're targeting a specific role, like a CIO, common useful hashtags include #CIO #ITDirector #Cloud #HybridCloud #BigData #AI #CognitiveComputing

#Storage #IoT #Collaboration #Productivity and #FutureOfWork.

- If you're in a field like wellness or mindfulness, use hashtags such as #Wellness #WholenessAtWork #Mindfulness #NLP #MindfulnessInBusiness #SelfLeadership and #Meditation.

❑ **I've identified 6-8 hashtags**: Between your company, your industry or area of thought leadership, your role, topics that are relevant to these and the topics that interest you, you'll crack this one. Here they are:

1. _____

2. _____

3. _____

4. _____

5. _____

6. _____

7. _____

8. _____

9 INCLUDE
PEOPLE, BUSINESSES, AND PUBLICATIONS IN YOUR POSTS

Social media is all about engaging in conversations and growing your community. In addition to using hashtags to draw people and companies to you, you should integrate publications and communities wherever it's relevant to do so.

Let's talk about tagging. I don't mind being tagged in posts sometimes, but there is also a *lot* of nonsense going on. Social media etiquette is an unspoken agreement between us, and tagging people is one of its finest arts.

When you tag someone, you put the responsibility on the person tagged to interact with the post. Most people will feel a strong sense of obligation to respond. We're human, and that's a lovely trait of humanity. These interactions can be engaging and enriching both for participants and the larger community. But tagging—and the obligation it creates—should not be taken too far.

Here's an example. If you're sharing an article from *Fortune Magazine*, use @Fortune to find the publication's LinkedIn profile and copy it into your post. (If *Fortune* didn't have a LinkedIn page, it wouldn't come up as an option to tag.) Make sure you select the right entity from the drop-down list that appears—see the image below.

You can do the same on other social sites too, including Facebook and Twitter.

Using @ to **tag** a person or organization is called "at-mentioning".

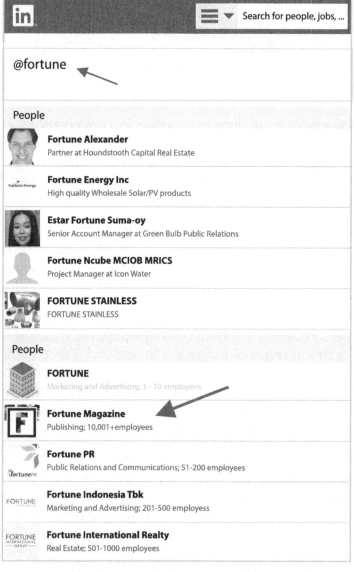

Figure 19. Use @ to find people and organizations

Another example: if your friend publishes a great blog post and you share it, use @ again and type that friend's name. This will bring them up as an option to tag in your post, which gives them the opportunity to engage with you, or at least thank you for sharing their post.

The first rule of etiquette you need to keep in mind is that tagging—like most aspects of social media—is all about reciprocity. If you want to draw people to you, you must also draw nearer to others. It's about interaction—the collective versus the self. (That's the *social* bit of social media.) It makes me crazy when a contact tags me in everything they post, but they never once interact with what *I* share. If you use tagging as a one-way-street, don't be surprised to find it's a dead end.

So, if you insist on tagging people in your posts, do them the courtesy of interacting with their posts too—whether they tag you or not. I rarely tag anyone because I hate to annoy my community with excessive tagging. (And let's be honest, it really can be annoying.)

If you're promoting a commercial deal, running an event, or selling something, why not drop your contacts a personal note and ask them if they'd be willing to support you rather than tagging them in a post? Personal contact is always better received.

And what about tagging famous (or infamous) people? I'm talking about people like Bill Gates, who gets tagged all the time. I've seen at least 10 people in my LinkedIn network do it recently. Now, you *can* tag Bill Gates and any number of other big names, but *should* you?

Think about this man and his busy day. Do you *really* think he will see what you are sharing? I am sure he has a very busy assistant going through his accounts so he can respond to the ones that matter. Put yourself in his shoes. He's trying to solve some of the biggest challenges the world faces. Do you think he has time to respond to everyone tagging him? Is your post worthy of his attention, or are you just trying to call attention to yourself through digital name-dropping?

Indiscriminate tagging is a nightmare for non-celebrities, too. When executives feel overwhelmed through over-tagging and the mindless messages filling their inboxes, they'll quit the very platforms you're trying to attract them on!

In short, think before you tag. If you don't have a *very* good reason to tag someone, especially a public figure, please don't do it. It makes you look silly, it's counter-productive, and it diminishes the effectiveness of LinkedIn as a connectivity platform.

❑ **I promise to tag people and businesses when I share.** I also promise not to tag famous people just to do so. I'll tag with agreement when they are colleagues or professional friends.

10 SEND

TWO RECOMMENDATIONS TODAY

Recommendations are important, and you should always seek recommendations for the work you are proud of. We all know how precious time is these days, so when a busy person takes the time to write a recommendation for you, it says a lot about you and your work.

Make a list of the people you want to ask for recommendations. How can you help *them* recommend you? Obviously, you can send a request and hope for the best. But if you outline what they could emphasize and suggest a few things for them to craft into their own language, they're more likely to respond with something pointed and useful. It's natural to feel uncomfortable doing this, but look at it this way: you're making it easy for them to help you (which they want to do) and showing respect for *their* time, which is very important.

The best way to get recommendations is to proactively write recommendations for the people you put on the list you made below. Reciprocity makes the world go around. Most people who receive a thoughtful recommendation from you will respond in kind with recommendations. If they need prompting, go to your *edit profile* page, scroll down to the recommendations section and click on the tab in the right, **ask to be recommended**.

It's simple but you must be persistent, because this is very important for your career. One effective strategy is to ask people, via some other means, before you send the request on LinkedIn. This small personal gesture will give you a much stronger chance of a response—people really appreciate a little bit of courtesy. If you are looking for a job and really need recommendations, go ahead and mention this. Sometimes you need to light a fire under the people who want to help you. Don't wait for them to act; get on it!

When it comes to people whose recommendations really matter to you, don't be afraid to nag them. It's a big gift we can give when we support each other's careers and ambitions. Make sure you respond in kind to anyone who takes the time to write a recommendation for you. Get out there and recommend as many of your professional connections as you can. They will be delighted to receive a recommendation from you, and we can change the culture of apathy one connection at a time.

Social media is definitely a place where you gain more if you give more. Be a giver!

Notes—People I want to recommend and people I'd love a recommendation from:

_____

_____

_____

_____

_____

_____

❏ **I've written and sent two recommendations.** It's good to give!

11 LIST YOUR SKILLS

If you haven't already done this, make a list of your skills. Under your *edit profile* section, click on the **add skills** button. You can add up to 50 skills—and the best bit is that a window drops down with suggestions of skills you might add. If you enter "marketing," it will give you every variation of marketing you could list, thus making it very easy to get to 50. But should you really list 50 skills?

Before we discuss how many skills you should list, you might be wondering how important the LinkedIn **skills section is in the first place.** Know that recruiters now have the option of searching for and narrowing down candidates by their skills—LinkedIn Skills, that is. This section is only going to become more important.

Today LinkedIn Skills appears when you are viewing someone's profile. When it appears, you're asked if the connection knows anything about three suggested skills. To provide this endorsement, all you need to do is click yes and it's done. This appears in their profile, and it's the easiest way to provide a recommendation for a colleague or someone you admire.

Although, recently, I have noticed LinkedIn is asking for more information on your knowledge of the person and the skills, which means skills will be even more important, as they have an additional layer of validation now.

However, the skills that hit 99+ are the ones that register in the big SEO database of LinkedIn, the ones that have a true impact. Your goal is to get your core skills endorsed over 99 times, and then you will rank higher in searches for people with these skills.

The best strategy is to select your top three skills, which you pin at the top of your skills section. You will notice a visual of a pin – make sure your most important skills are pinned. Once these skills reach 99+, move it down and move another important skill into the top three.

And enhancing our search standings is an important part of effectively using LinkedIn. Your highest-ranked skills demonstrate to interested parties (including recruiters) that this is an area of expertise for you. If you're too lazy to write recommendations—*and admit it, some of you are*—this is the next best thing. Tick those boxes when they pop up and help your friends, peers, and community be more successful. But make sure you have your key skills checked as well.

Now, go back and review the skills you have listed on LinkedIn. Are they outdated? Can you delete some? If you have hit 99+ it is probably worth keeping the skill, but when it comes to those skills that are no longer relevant or have landed you few endorsements, consider deleting them. Make sure you have 10 core skills that you want to get to the magic number, 99+. The best way to get people ticking yes to your skills, is to tick those skills for others. Remember what we said about reciprocity? Get on it.

Notes—Skills I want to profile:

_____

_____

_____

_____

_____

_____

_____

❑ **I've looked at five other people whom I know
and endorsed their skills.** It's good to give!

12 ARE YOU
LOOKING FOR A JOB?

You'll get the most out of LinkedIn if you help LinkedIn help you. When you are in your own profile, under your banner, LinkedIn asks if you are open to job opportunities. Click on this to see the job tab. You have a space to fill in your preferences. These include where you live and the cities where you are interested in working, the job level you are looking for, which industries you want to work in, as well as what size company you want to work for. One way you can make LinkedIn work for you is by giving it as much information as you can to ensure it is feeding you with the best roles available. If I was looking for work, this is the first thing I would do.

You should also upgrade to **Job Seeker Premium**, especially if you are serious about looking for work. Premium is costly, but when you are looking for a new job, it is an investment worth making. I'll have more to say about Premium later.

In August 2016, LinkedIn launched its **Open Candidates** mode. This handy feature is an opportunity to *privately* signal to recruiters that you are open to new opportunities. You can find this option on the preferences in your LinkedIn job home page, and all you have to do is turn it on and fill in the information. Don't worry, your company (and the recruiters associated with your company) will not see the signal that you are looking. Connections of mine who have used this feature tell me they have had incredible results.

Another often-missed tool is the **LinkedIn Job Search App**.

In the recruitment and job seeker area on LinkedIn, there are always new developments with LinkedIn. Stay up to date on what is happening, because it is a fabulous platform to help you get where you want to be.

Though LinkedIn is so much more than a recruitment tool, that aspect of it remains a critical core strength of the platform. If you are looking for a new job, make sure you use LinkedIn to its full potential.

13 USE LINKEDIN GROUPS

LinkedIn Groups are a terrific resource that you should not ignore. You can join up to 100 groups; however, it is impossible to participate actively and intelligently across all of them, so be very selective! I recommend choosing a maximum of 10 that are relevant to you. And even then, if you can participate effectively in more than three, you obviously have too much time on your hands ☺.

When you're deciding which groups to join, go to the *Groups* tab, and search for groups aligned to your profession. You'll find the *Groups* tab under the *Work* button at the top of your LinkedIn profile page.

Another easy way to find groups is to enter "groups" in the LinkedIn search window and click on the link that appears. This search will also give you recommendations for groups aligned to your profile, which can be very handy for finding relevant ones to join.

As a best practice, I recommend focusing on groups organized according to three themes:

1.   Geographic: people near you

2.   Specific position: people who have the same job as you

3.   Industry: people in your industry

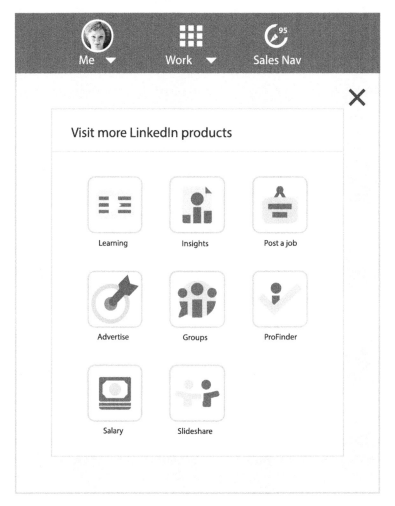

Figure 20. Finding Groups in *more LinkedIn products*

When you join groups, you can indicate how often you want to be notified of group activities. For groups in which you want to be really engaged, tick the daily email, but for the rest, tick *weekly email* or the *no email notification at all* option. The more groups you join, the more overwhelming these emails can be. Group posts now appear in your LinkedIn feed, a recent change which I believe helps encourage more participation.

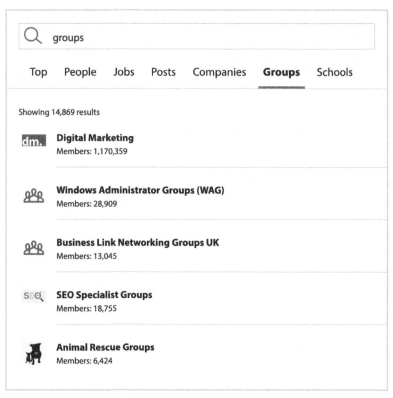

Figure 21. Search for Groups

Another option to find the right groups is to ask your peers, customers, partners, and other influencers in your field where they are. What groups do they value? Where do they get the best insights? All group activity is now private, so you can only see what is going on in a group after you have joined. It's hard to gauge what is valuable in advance, so asking around is a way to save you time and get you to the most relevant groups for your profession.

Once you've joined a group, carefully monitor it and see how other members are participating. Some people will advise you to blast all of your groups with information, such as your blog posts. I completely disagree with this strategy. Sure, you can build a profile by getting your name out there, but at what cost to your credibility? For many people, including the executives I work with, aggressive self-promotion is fundamentally against what effective, meaningful social leadership is all about. If you want to win hearts and minds, be very careful about annoying your audience—even when you see other people doing it.

So, **go easy on the self-promotion**. A more subtle way to get your content out there is to find a buddy (or a team of buddies) who promote your work, and you post theirs to return the favor.

How useful are LinkedIn Groups, really?

Once you've started using and participating in various groups, you can be your own judge of their usefulness for you. Many people find them to be too spammy, depending on how participants in their groups operate and self-promote.

Personally, I'm turned off by the fact that group alerts are sent by email. I already have enough emails to read. Group updates appearing in your feed, as I mentioned above, is a promising new development, but at the time of this writing, LinkedIn Groups is still not an ideal experience. I'm part of more professional groups on Facebook, where I find the simpler model and notification system easier to manage.

With that said, some industries, such as construction, energy and gas, operate almost exclusively through LinkedIn Groups. Real business is happening there daily. It's important to understand the power of LinkedIn Groups for *your* industry. If that's where the action is happening, that's where you need to be. There is no one-size-fits-all approach to LinkedIn Groups, and you can certainly make the best of the ones where you choose to participate.

Notes—Types of groups I want to join:

_____

_____

_____

_____

❑ **I've applied to three groups.**

14 LIST
THE CAUSES YOU CARE ABOUT AND PROMOTE THE ONES YOU VOLUNTEER FOR

LinkedIn gives you the option, when you're building your profile, to list the causes you volunteer for and care about. This is a small section, but do spend time on it. Even if you are not actively participating in any causes, you can still list what you care about. This gives future customers, partners, employees, and employers insight into the sort of person you are.

You've already noticed that many people are on social media to promote themselves, sell products, or just bore the pants off everyone around them. But great social media participation is much more than that, and a lot of being a meaningful leader, regardless of the platform, comes down to what you give to your audience. You share great information because you think the people who follow you will value it. You create great content so you can share the things you are learning or experiencing. This is the fundamental power of social media.

It's about our collective humanity—which means that small things like the volunteer experience and the causes section are important to share, and I recommend spending the time to make this section of your LinkedIn profile as strong as any other.

We bring our whole self to work today. This is part of owning that.

Notes—Causes and Volunteering over the years:

_____

_____

_____

_____

_____

_____

_____

❏ **I've added these to my LinkedIn Profile.**

15 HAVE YOU BEEN PUBLISHED ANYWHERE?

Under the *Publications* section in your profile, you can add any content you've created and published somewhere else. If you have been published anywhere beyond your blog (academic papers, whitepapers, ebooks, guest articles, etc.) include these to help build a complete profile of who you are, what you stand for, and what you've achieved.

LinkedIn has changed dramatically over the years and there are many ways to feature your published work. Adding it here is a simple process, and adds weight to your overall profile. The more sections you fill out on LinkedIn, the greater the chance to get to all-star status.

The published section appears under your accomplishments, and looks like this:

Accomplishments

13 **Publications**
What is the definition of content marketing? Agency bosses give their verdict · Can Companies Overcome Asia's Digital Media Challenge · Find Your Perfect B2B Content Partner · A Dragon Hunt in Singapore's Chinatown · Are Corporate Values Still Relevant or Cliched? · How Asian Companies use Social Media · Asia's Pacific Content Trends - Stay Local or go Global? · Crafting an Internal Communications Strategy · Managing Asia the Microsoft Way · Go Social or Die...

Figure 22. Accomplishments and publications on LinkedIn

Notes—I've been published in:

_____

_____

_____

_____

_____

_____

_____

_____

❑ **I've added these to my profile.**

16 ADD
HONORS, AWARDS, AND ASSOCIATIONS

What **awards and recognition have your achievements earned you**? Even if you are at the beginning of your career, look to your past and find what is valuable to mention in this section. These can be global awards or more local recognition. Whatever you have been recognized for, make sure it is linked to your professional profile—these things matter. Also, don't forget that internal awards are great to include as well. Keep this section updated as the awards flow in.

Additionally, what **professional associations** are you involved in? Make sure you list any professional associations as you join them, and if the association is on LinkedIn, you can link your profile to it. If you are on an executive committee or have a non-executive role, say so. Anyone who has been part of an association knows and respects what a commitment this entails. Make sure you let your audience know about it. This section is primarily for professional pursuits, but if you are a member of charitable associations, include them here, too.

Notes—List of my associations:

_____

_____

_____

_____

List of my awards:

_____

_____

_____

_____

❏ **I've added both to my profile.**

Let's talk about whether you should pay for Premium membership, especially if your company doesn't offer it to you. In my experience, few companies offer Premium subscriptions to their employees. Typically, only people in sales benefit from paid services like Sales Navigator.

This is a huge missed opportunity, because paid accounts empower employees to dig deeper on LinkedIn. In today's world virtually everyone is in sales and marketing, and the idea that only certain employees get access to the best tools is something that needs to change. The challenge is that companies often still believe that only sales people touch the customer, something we know is not true. Companies should invest in and encourage employees who are engaged on LinkedIn by paying for Premium membership.

In the meantime, basic LinkedIn is free, but consider upgrading to Premium membership. Here are a few benefits of being a Premium member:

- A Premium membership means you appear higher in searches when people are looking for professionals with your skills.

- You can find more people.

- Your profile is more visible.

- Apart from people who appear anonymously (**don't be one of those people**), you can see more information on who has been viewing your profile.

- When you are prospecting for new business leads, you have more criteria options with which to search.

- Premium membership gives you InMail access, which means you can connect and exchange with people who are not your first degree connections.

In addition to all of the above, investing in yourself through a Premium upgrade demonstrates that you take the platform seriously—an essential consideration if you want to make the most of what LinkedIn can do for your career.

❏ **I'm Premium.**

18 FINAL
TIPS ON LINKEDIN

If you do everything I've suggested so far, you're going to have an impressive and effective profile—we're aiming for **all-star,** right? However, don't think you can do it once, tick that box, and move on.

Keep going back to refresh images and links and update your content. The internet is dynamic and always evolving. Static is stagnant, and your LinkedIn profile should be neither.

Some suggestions for a dynamic profile:

- Make sure your education information is up to date and link your learning institution to your profile. If a school still exists and has a LinkedIn page, it will come up as a linking option.

- If you work on a major project with a team of people (and it isn't top secret), add the title of the project with a quick summary and link to the profiles of team members involved in the project. This means the project description will appear on their profiles too, and it's a powerful way to connect professionals to each other.

- LinkedIn lets you provide advice on **making contact** with you. My profile says: "Make sure it's appropriate and if you want to pitch something to me, tell me why you've targeted me in the first instance. I'll read it if you can justify why you thought I'd be a good contact." Most people will ignore this kind of disclaimer, but it's important to be proactive about the kind of communication you want.

- Listing languages in which you are proficient is a must!

- LinkedIn's video features—including live video— are an effective way to promote your thought leadership or the work you are doing.

- Keep an eye on **ProFinder** if you plan to freelance or if you expect to utilize freelance talent. The gig economy is upon us, and this service is an important addition to LinkedIn.

- Finally, always be looking for new updates to LinkedIn. This powerful platform is a constant work in progress and great new options are constantly being developed.

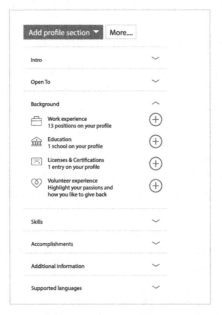

Figure 23. Adding more sections to your profile

Be Amazing

Using social media like an all-star pro is about sharing your knowledge and passion with your community—no matter your topic or focus. There is an audience for every subject, after all. The important attitude is to remember it is more about what you give than what you get. Becoming a powerful social leader is an **act of service.** How can you serve your community and make it better, smarter, and more successful? It's not about you. **It's never been about you**, and that is a message any social media cynic (you know who you are) can appreciate.

Don't throw the baby out with that bathwater, even if you've been turned off by self-promoting behavior on social media. We are all competing globally today, and the fact that the loudest voices can drown out many quieter, more valuable voices is a defining challenge of our time. Be a part of the solution by building a strong social leadership position as an act of service, versus the self-serving approach more common today. It's a fine line understanding the difference. However, if you can embrace the idea of service as central to your social leadership presence, we'll all be one step closer to making our corporate online world a more positively connected and empowering place.

Engaging in a global platform and giving of yourself in this way—and doing it well—means you will receive so much in return: professional opportunities, new communities, speaking invitations, new customers, personal growth opportunities, trust, loyalty, and the feeling of impacting many lives for the better.

It's critical to be a positive force on social media. Disagreeing with someone is fine, but be constructive in your criticism and open to opposing views. Have a conversation, not an argument. No one wins a social media argument, anyway. Don't feed the trolls!

It's important to participate by supporting and celebrating others in your field. However, be very wary of overdoing your participation. On LinkedIn in particular, people *switch off from* connections who are annoyingly overactive. We are asking our audience for too much time invested in us. And with the dirge of information available, it is hard to get that much time from people. Do less and be awesome.

I recommend not posting more than once a day (or once a week or month—consistency is what matters). Your time is very valuable, and not over-posting should help you manage how much time you spend on social media. It is more effective to show up less often in your contacts' news feeds but to be world-class every time you do.

When you share your own content (blogs, videos, etc.) you are asking your audience to do you a favor—to give you their time. When you share other people's content that's aligned to the topics you care most about, you are doing your audience a favor—finding valuable, world-class information for them so they don't have to find it themselves. Our goal, as social leaders, is to become a one-stop-shop in our area of expertise. Spend most of your social media time sharing quality content from other people and participating meaningfully in conversations. Contribute this way, and occasionally ask for your followers' time with your own content. They will not mind giving it to you when you have served them so well.

We've reached a point of content shock and saturation today. Social media should not be a megaphone for your views. If you want to be heard at all, aim to be excellent by adding value, lifting people up, engaging in discussions, and boosting your community to make everyone a champion.

It's also critical to focus on earning people's respect and trust, but you must be patient. It really can take a long time to build your profile and credibility, especially if you are still coming up through the ranks of your profession.

Finally, be critical of the advice you get—and that even goes for what I am writing here. If it doesn't resonate with you and who *you* are, find your own way. There is no one right way to be successful on social media. Listen to others but listen to yourself first and trust in your own judgment—it's rarely wrong, when you really listen to it.

Things You Can Do to Keep Lifting Your Profile

The steps I've outlined are a starting point in helping you become successful on LinkedIn by creating a compelling profile. If you implement these 18 things now, it will help you establish your presence and become confident in your participation. These are only some of the things I've learned, and LinkedIn is changing all the time. I've invested deeply in various social platforms and blogs over the last decade, and these recommendations come from working with thousands of professionals on their social leadership skills. The first question I always get is *where do I start?* Start with the 18 points we've discussed, then consider my six final steps below. See these as a bonus!

Six more things for over-achievers:

1. Define who you are and what you want to be known for. Tie your social voice to your heart and get your focus clear, because this is how you make an impact and build a strong brand. If you don't know where to start, ask the people closest to you: *What am I good at? What is my passion? What makes me stand out in a crowd? What is my gift to the world?*

2. Define your social channels, start with LinkedIn if you are a professional. Make sure you have complete profiles across all channels. It takes time to do a great job at this. Which channels should you use? You should be where your customers are, but you should also be on social media platforms *you* enjoy. This is critical. Keep in mind you can learn to enjoy them over time, too. I hated Twitter when I started, and now I love it.

3. Identify the content resources you can rely on for knowledge and inspiration today (*Harvard Business Review*, *The New York Times*, BBC, TED Talks, etc.) and then make a commitment to sharing one article or video a week—everyone can do that! If you loved something or it inspired you, don't you think someone else would value it too? When you share any information, always add your opinion to the post. This is where you deliver value to your audience. Sharing content without offering a nugget of interpretation is a wasted opportunity. People are looking to cut through the noise of social media and to overcome content shock, so you can help them do that by guiding them to your content through your words.

4. Can you start blogging? Is it in you? Maybe video is your thing, or podcasting? If you decide to blog, get started by publishing articles on LinkedIn, and then build your own blogging platform (using Wordpress, for example) or launch a YouTube channel. Once you know you're committed to content creation, why not launch your own professional website? If you're not sure what to talk about when you begin creating your own content, start by answering the questions you get

asked the most and add a unique layer of insight in your answers. Once you start, you will be amazed at how the ideas for future content will flow through you.

5. Don't think about what you will get; focus on giving and supporting as the priority. Give, give, give to receive, and the wins will come. Join the Giving Economy—the idea that you become a social leader to help others be successful. You will feel good and add meaning to your personal brand—and the fastest way to build your brand is by being a champion of your community. The people who succeed the most are driven to create change in their field. It is this drive that ensures success, not how you compare to anyone else. What change do you want to see in the world? Become a voice for that change in the #GivingEconomy.

6. Be brave enough to make mistakes, get stuck in, find your way, work it out, learn, grow, and excel. Some people are intimidated by social media. If you define your story, define your audience, then define the social media channels best suited to sharing your story and the content and opinions you want to be known for, you will already be miles ahead of many others in your field. It's hard putting yourself out there—I know this from experience—so prepare yourself, have a goal, and get started. Then evolve as you go. Define what success means for *you*, then chart your own unique path to get there.

Thank you so much for reading this book. I am incredibly passionate about the opportunity we all have, through social leadership to fundamentally shift our world for the better by linking to each other. I'm passionate about our collective power and I hope my words inspire you to join in.

Set aside your limiting self-beliefs and take this chance to be a powerful and positive force on social media. We need your voice and your vision, so it's time to step up and be excellent.

Cheers,

Andrea

Andrea T Edwards, CSP

Andrea T Edwards CSP, the Digital Conversationalist, is a communications evangelist and expert in content marketing, social leadership, and employee advocacy.

Working with brands to help them embrace the voice of their employees, Andrea sees empowering employees to be social leaders as the cornerstone of business transformation today. Empowered employees who are social leaders and content creators in their own right delight customers, enjoy more exciting career opportunities, are more engaged and loyal to their employers, are externally focused and better connected within their industries, and—through the collective power of their voices—drive business growth and attract the best talent.

A globally award-winning B2B communications professional with more than 20 years' experience, Andrea is a content marketing strategy pioneer, best-selling author, blogger, writer, and trainer/coach for businesses and professionals around the world. A certified speaking professional (CSP) discussing content marketing and social leadership, Andrea works with the world's largest companies on the transformation needed within to maximize business growth in our digital age.

Andrea has deep experience in the technology sector and has worked in defense, aerospace, government, travel and tourism, HR, the environment, professional services, healthcare, marketing services, market research, financial services, insurance, engineering, manufacturing, and even the brewing industry!

A blogger for more than a decade and widely recognized as a B2B content marketing and social media influencer, Andrea is a travel junkie who's had the privilege to work around the world—across Europe, the US, ANZ, and Asia.

Acknowledgements

A book like this is based on passion and uncompromising belief in your ideas combined with decades of experience through a lot of ups and downs! My thanks for the leaders in Microsoft, IBM, BNP Paribas Securities Services, and many more for trusting me, taking a risk with these ideas, and partnering with me to prove that social leadership is a powerful tool for business transformation and can deliver huge results for any business professional. You have all helped me hone these ideas into the 18 steps I've outlined in this book.

Many thanks to Stanimira Koleva (my first executive champion), Tiffani Bova, Nishan Weerasinghe, Michelle Cockrill, Julian Kasparian, Wendy McEwan, Sinisa Nikolic, Thariyan Chacko, Shalaka Verma, Eric Schnatterly, Deepthi Anne, James Taylor, Andrew Bryant, Jerome Joseph, Pamela Wigglesworth, Kevin Cottam, John Gordon, Lindsay Adams, Warwick Merry, Kerrie Phipps, Cathy Johnson, Karen Leong, and Natalie Turner—legends all. An extra shout out to Anne Phey, Sunny Panjabi and Tara Cremin-Moody too. You three have been amazing supporters of my work. Thanks as well to Natasha David for her early editing work.

I definitely wouldn't have gotten this book across the line without Joanne Flinn, whose Project Wings Author Services got my book strategy clear and pulled together over a hundred pieces—in record swift time. Thanks so much, Joanne, you amazing professional, for taking the pressure of a book not done off my back. Now it's live and helping people unleash their voices. The truth is, we need the humble, the introspective, the intelligent, the passionate, and the givers to step into their voices. When this happens, we can collectively make the world a better place!

I want to thank one of the most important women in my life, Vicky Minguillo aka Aunty Vick. Not only did you teach me how to be a better mother, but you've given me the most valuable gift to chase my dreams – time. I love and honour you sister from another mother.

Finally, a huge thanks to the men in my life. My husband Steve Johnson—you believed in me while enduring the journey (during which I wasn't always pleasant to be around) and never wavered in your support for me though you didn't always agree with how I wanted to go about things. You are perfect for me. And thanks to my boys, Lex and Jax. You let me travel for my work without making me feel too guilty about it, and I've got to tell you, it's the cutest thing watching you look at my YouTube channels. I know what I talk about is boring for you, maybe one day, you'll understand what it was all about.

Love youse all! xxxxx

Made in the USA
Coppell, TX
01 January 2021